PHILIPPIANS

THE TEACHER'S OUTLINE & STUDY BIBLE

Student's Journal

PHILIPPIANS

THE TEACHER'S OUTLINE & STUDY BIBLE

Student's Journal

NEW TESTAMENT

KING JAMES VERSION

Leadership Ministries Worldwide
PO Box 21310
Chattanooga, TN 37424-0310

The Teacher's Outline & Study Bible is written for God's people to use both in their personal lives and in their teaching. Leadership Ministries Worldwide wants God's people to use The Teacher's Outline & Study Bible. The purpose of the copyright is to prevent the reproduction, misuse, and abuse of the material.

May our Lord bless us all as we live, preach, teach, and write for Him, fulfilling His great commission to live righteous and godly lives and to make disciples of all nations.

Please address all requests for information or permission to:

Leadership Ministries Worldwide
PO Box 21310
Chattanooga TN 37424-0310
Ph.# (423) 855-2181 FAX (423) 855-8616 E-Mail 74152.616@compuserve.com
http://www.outlinebible.org

Library of Congress Catalog Card Number: 94-073070
International Standard Book Number: 0-945863-45-4

PRINTED IN THE U.S.A.

PUBLISHED BY LEADERSHIP MINISTRIES WORLDWIDE

HOW TO USE

THE TEACHER'S OUTLINE AND STUDY BIBLE (TOSB)
STUDENT'S JOURNAL

To gain maximum benefit, here is all you do. Follow these easy steps, using the sample outline below.

1 STUDY TITLE

2 MAJOR POINTS

3 SUB-POINTS

4 STUDY THE WORD OF GOD AS FOLLOWS:

	B. The Steps to Peace (Part II): Prayer & Positive Thinking, 4:6-9
1. Peace comes through prayer a. The charge: Do not worry or be anxious b. The remedy: Prayer 1) About everything 2) With requests 3) With thanksgiving c. The promise: Peace 1) Peace that passes all understanding 2) Peace that keeps our hearts & minds	6 Be careful for nothing; but in ev- ery thing by pray- er and supplica- tion with thanksgiving let your requests be made known unto God. 7 And the peace of God, which passeth all understanding, shall keep your hearts and minds through Christ Jesus.
2. Peace comes through positive thinking a. The charge: Think & practice things that are... 1) True 2) Honest 3) Just 4) Pure	8 Finally, brethren, whatsoever things are true, whatsoever things are honest, whatsoever things are just, whatsoever things are pure, whatsoever things are lovely, what-

1. First: Read the **Study Title** two or three times so that the subject sinks in.
2. Second: Read the **Study Title** and the **Major Points** (Pts.1,2,3) together quickly. Do this several times and you will quickly grasp the overall subject.
3. Third: Read both the **Major Points** and **Sub-Points**. Do this slower than Step 2. Note how the points are beside the applicable verse, and simply state what the Scripture is saying—in Outline form.
4. Fourth: Read the **Aim** and **Introduction**. Then read and re-read the Scripture and Outline points. Pray that the Holy Spirit will sharpen your focus on exactly what the Scripture is saying. Next, jot down what you see in the Scripture as you study each point. (Space is provided under each point for your note.)

STUDENTS, PLEASE NOTE:

Take some time every day--just a few minutes if that is all you have--and do the following:

⇒ Read and re-read the **Scripture** and the **Major Points** over and over, time and again, day by day throughout the week. Drive the **Scripture** and **Major Points** into your heart and mind.

(Please continue on next page)

⇒ Write down your own thoughts, exactly what you see in the Scripture as you study each point. (As stated above, space is provided under each point for your notes.) By doing this, you will have your own personal commentary on this particular book when you are finished--a treasure to keep and refer back to throughout your life.
⇒ When the lesson is taught, listen closely for the voice of the Holy Spirit as He speaks from the Bible through your teacher. Add to your own personal notes as your teacher expounds on the Scripture.

BE A GOOD STEWARD OF YOUR TIME...
⇒ by being prepared to learn.
⇒ by praying for your teacher--that God would use him/her to clearly explain the Scriptures.
⇒ by sharing insights gained for your own study time.
⇒ by taking good notes while the lesson is being taught.
⇒ by recording your reflections after the lesson has been taught. At the close of every lesson, there is space for you to record whatever decision you have made for Christ and any thoughts about how you can apply the lesson to your life. As you study through the Bible, you will find these comments invaluable as you walk in Christ day by day.

PLEASE NOTE: It is of utmost importance that you grasp the Scripture, the Study Title, and Major Points. It is this that the Holy Spirit will make alive to your heart and that you will more likely remember and use day by day.

REMEMBER!

The Teacher's Outline & Study Bible - Student's Takeaway is the only study material that actually outlines the Bible verse by verse for you right beside the Scripture. As you accumulate the various books of this series for your study, you will have the Bible outlined book by book, passage by passage, and verse by verse.

The outlines alone make saving every book a must! Over the course of your life, you will have your very own personalized commentary of the Bible. No other book will mean as much to you because it will contain your insights, your struggles, your victories, and your recorded moments with the Lord.

"Study to show thyself approved unto God, a workman that needeth not to be ashamed, rightly dividing the word of truth" (2 Tim.2:15).

"All scripture is given by inspiration of God, and is profitable for doctrine, for reproof, for correction, for instruction in righteousness: that the man of God may be perfect, throughly furnished unto all good works" (2 Tim.3:16-17).

Now, may our wonderful Lord bless you mightily as you study His Holy Word. And may our Lord grant you much fruit: the reaching of many who will become greater servants and witnesses for Him.

LEADERSHIP MINISTRIES WORLDWIDE

Publisher & Distributor of...

The Preacher's Outline & Sermon Bible

DEDICATED:

To all the men and women of the world who study and teach the Gospel of our Lord Jesus Christ
and
To the Mercy and Grace of God.

&

- Demonstrated to us in Christ Jesus our Lord.

"In whom we have redemption through His blood, the forgiveness of sins, according to the riches of His grace." (Eph. 1:7)

- Out of the mercy and grace of God His Word has flowed. Let every person know that God will have mercy upon him, forgiving and using him to fulfill His glorious plan of salvation.

"For God so loved the world, that he gave his only begotten Son, that whosoever believeth in him should not perish, but have everlasting life. For God sent not his Son into the world to condemn the world; but that the world through him might be saved." (John 3:16-17)

"For this is good and acceptable in the sight of God our Saviour; who will have all men to be saved, and to come unto the knowledge of the truth." (I Tim. 2:3-4)

&

The Teacher's Outline & Study Bible
is written for God's people to use
in their study and teaching of God's Holy Word.

OUTLINE OF PHILIPPIANS

THE TEACHER'S OUTLINE & STUDY BIBLE **- Student's Takeaway** is *unique*. It differs from all other Study Bibles in that every Passage and Subject is outlined right beside the Scripture. When you choose any *Subject* below and turn to the reference, you have not only the Scripture, but you discover the Scripture and Subject *already outlined for you—verse by verse*.

For a quick example, choose one of the subjects below and turn over to the Scripture—you will find this to be a marvelous help for faster, easier, and more meaningful study of Scripture.

A suggestion: For the quickest overview of Philippians, first read *all the major titles* (I, II, III, etc.), then come back and read the subtitles.

OUTLINE OF PHILIPPIANS

THE EPISTLE OF PAUL THE APOSTLE TO THE

PHILIPPIANS

INTRODUCTION

AUTHOR: Paul, the Apostle.

Clement of Rome, who lived in the first century, wrote a letter to the Corinthians and referred to Paul's letter to the Philippians. Polycarp, who lived in the second century, wrote the Philippians and mentioned Paul's letter. Ignatius, another early church leader, alluded to it. There are other references to Paul's authorship by Irenaeus, Clement of Alexandria, and Tertullian--all early church writers (Ralph P. Martin. *The Epistle of Paul to the Philippians.* "Tyndale Bible Commentaries," ed. by RVG Tasker. Grand Rapids, MI: Eerdmans, 1959, p.28, 36).

DATE: Uncertain. Probably somewhere around A.D. 60-63 while Paul was in prison at Rome.

TO WHOM WRITTEN: "To all the saints in Jesus Christ which are at Philippi, with the bishops and deacons" (Ph.1:1). The message is applicable to all the saints of every church.

PURPOSE: Paul wrote Philippians for several reasons.

1. He wished to prevent any criticism against a very dear friend and servant of Christ, Epaphroditus. Epaphroditus had been sent by the Philippian church to deliver a gift and to encourage Paul while he was a prisoner in Rome. But Epaphroditus became extremely sick, almost to the point of death, while with Paul. His return to Philippi was delayed, apparently for a long time. Because of this, Paul feared criticism of Epaphroditus by the church. They might think he was a weakling or a quitter. So Paul wrote to ease the path for Epaphroditus and to prevent any criticism of him (Ph.2:25-30).
2. Paul wished to thank the Philippian church for its help throughout his ministry. They had sent him a gift right after he had founded the church and moved on (Ph.1:5; 4:15; 2 Cor.8:1f). They had also sent gifts to him at Thessalonica (Ph.4:16) and at Corinth (2 Cor.11:9). And now they sent him not only a gift, but even more, a dear, dear believer to minister to his needs while he was in prison (Ph.2:25-30; 4:18).
3. Paul wished to call the church to unity and harmony. There were two ladies who quarreled and were causing a disturbance (Ph.4:2; cp. 1:27; 2:2-4, 14). It was this disturbance that called forth one of the greatest pictures of Christ in the Holy Scriptures (Ph.2:5-11).
4. Paul wished to deal with some false teachers who were just beginning to arise in the church (Ph.3:2f).

SPECIAL FEATURES:

1. The City of Philippi. Philippi was the gateway to Europe. It lay on the great Roman road known as the Egnatian Way. The city was named after Philip of Macedonia, the father of Alexander the Great. The site was a natural fortress, sitting on a range of hills that separated Europe from Asia, the East from the West. The city was a strategic center commanding the great Egnatian Way.

Philippi was also a proud Roman colony. In fact, it was famous as a miniature Rome. A city became a Roman colony in one of two ways. At first Rome founded colonies throughout the outer reaches of the Empire to keep the peace and to guard against invasions from barbaric hordes. Veteran soldiers, ready for retirement, were usually granted citizenship if they would go out and settle these colonies. Later on, however, a city was granted the distinctive title of a Roman Colony for loyalty and service to the Empire. The distinctive thing about these colonies was their fanatic loyalty to Rome. The citizens kept all their Roman ties, the Roman language, titles, customs, affairs, and dress. They refused to allow any infiltration of local influence whatsoever. They totally rejected the influence of the world around them. They were Roman colonists within an alien environment.

The city of Philippi fit right into Paul's master plan. Its strategic location on the Egnatian Way assured the spread of the gospel throughout the Roman Empire. As Paul carried on his ministry, he was moving toward Rome and the regions beyond into Spain. He knew that the converts from Philippi, whose employment took them from Philippi throughout the Empire, could move on out ahead of him. The strong witness of businessmen and other new converts could reach the world for Christ far greater than he could by himself (cp. Acts 28:13f).

2. The Church at Philippi. Acts 16:1-40 describes the founding of the Philippian church on Paul's second missionary journey. It is one of the most exciting adventures in all of literature. Philippi witnessed the entrance of the gospel into Europe. Paul had made several attempts to go elsewhere, but the Holy Spirit prohibited him (Acts 16:6-7). Thus, he made his way to Troas, not really knowing why. While in Troas Paul experienced the incredible vision of a man in Macedonia crying out, "Come over and help us." Through that one vision, the Holy Spirit changed the cradle of society. He thrust Paul forth into Europe with the glorious gospel of Christianity, and since that day, the world has never been the same.

From Troas, Paul landed at the European or Macedonian port of Neapolis and immediately made his way to the strategic city of Philippi. When Paul arrived in Philippi he found what he called "a crooked and perverse generation" (Ph.2:15). He also found a small nucleous of women who had a Jewish background to which he could appeal. From this group there were two significant conversions: Lydia, a prominent business woman, and an unnamed slave girl who was possessed with a spirit of fortune-telling. Later on there was also a Roman jailer and his household who were converted. Paul was soon attacked and imprisoned and forced to leave Philippi. Consequently, the church had only a small beginning under Paul's personal leadership.

When Paul left, Luke remained with the handful of converts (Acts 17:1). The church met at Lydia's house and continued to grow (Acts 16:40). The converts came primarily from the pagan Gentile world (Ph.2:25; 4:2-3; Ro.15:26-27).

The strength of the Philippian church is seen in the fact that the church continued to support Paul throughout his ministry despite the little time he had with them. They supported him even while they themselves were suffering and being persecuted (cp. Ph.1:7, 27-30; 2:15; 3:10-11; 4:1). No wonder Paul called them "brethren dearly beloved and longed for, my joy and crown" (Ph.4:1) and boasted of them to other churches (2 Cor.8:1f).

3. Philippians is "The Most Personal of Paul's Epistles." It is written to a church dearly loved by the minister (cp. Ph.4:1).

4. Philippians is "The Epistle of Stewardship" (see Purpose, point 2).

5. Philippians is "The Epistle of Joy." The words "joy" and "rejoicing" are used sixteen times in four short chapters.

6. Philippians is "The Epistle That Stresses the Little Phrase 'In Christ' or 'In the Lord'." The whole thesis of Paul is that life is "*in Christ*" and that Christ is to be "*in life*" (cp. Ph.1:13, 14, 26, 29; 2:1, 5, 19, 24, 29; 3:1, 4, 9, 14; 4:1, 4, 6-7, 10, 13, 17, 21).

THE EPISTLE OF PAUL THE APOSTLE TO THE
PHILIPPIANS

	I. THE MARKS OF GOD'S PEOPLE, 1:1-30 **A. The Marks of a Healthy Church, 1:1-2** **CHAPTER 1**
1. A healthy church disciples young people **2. A healthy church serves Christ** **3. A healthy church is full of true saints** **4. A healthy church has leaders who lead by example** **5. A healthy church experiences grace & peace**	Paul and Timotheus, the servants of Jesus Christ, to all the saints in Christ Jesus which are at Philippi, with the bishops and deacons: 2 Grace be unto you, and peace, from God our Father, and from the Lord Jesus Christ.

Section I
THE MARKS OF GOD'S PEOPLE, Philippians 1:1-30

Study 1: THE MARKS OF A HEALTHY CHURCH

Text: Philippians 1:1-2

Aim: To do all you can to help build a healthy church.

Memory Verse:
"Grace be unto you, and peace, from God our Father, and from the Lord Jesus Christ" (Ph.1:2).

INTRODUCTION:
This is a most unusual greeting to a church from Paul. He does not refer to himself as an apostle of Jesus Christ. Why? There was no need for him to defend his call from God. His relationship with the church at Philippi was just what it should be: a relationship founded and rooted in Jesus Christ and in the love and respect for each other. The church held its minister, Paul, close to its heart; they loved and cared for him as few churches love and care for their ministers. This greeting gives some outstanding distinctives of a healthy church.

OUTLINE:
1. A healthy church disciples and nurtures young people (v.1).
2. A healthy church serves Christ (v.1).
3. A healthy church is full of true saints (v.1).
4. A healthy church has leaders who lead by example (v.1).
5. A healthy church experiences grace & peace (v.2).

PHILIPPIANS 1:1-2

PERSONAL OUTLINE NOTES

1. A HEALTHY CHURCH DISCIPLES AND NURTURES YOUNG PEOPLE (v.1).

2. A HEALTHY CHURCH SERVES CHRIST (v.1).

3. A HEALTHY CHURCH IS FULL OF TRUE SAINTS (v.1).

PHILIPPIANS 1:1-2

PERSONAL OUTLINE NOTES (continued)

4. A HEALTHY CHURCH HAS LEADERS WHO LEAD BY EXAMPLE (v.1).

5. A HEALTHY CHURCH EXPERIENCES GRACE AND PEACE (v.2)

SUMMARY

As you have gone through this study, you have seen the foundations of a healthy church getting a little bit clearer. It takes time to develop into a healthy church. Pray for your church; give yourself to its mission by getting involved and by living out these five important points:

1. Nurture and disciple young people.
2. Be a slave of Jesus Christ.
3. Live as a saint should live.
4. Be a leader who leads by example.
5. Make sure you have truly experienced God's grace and peace, then become a vessel of God's grace and peace to others.

PHILIPPIANS 1:1-2

PERSONAL JOURNAL NOTES
(Reflection & Response)

1. The most important thing that I learned from this lesson was:

2. The area that I need to work on the most is:

3. I can apply this lesson to my life by:

4. Closing statement of commitment:

Outline	Scripture	Scripture (cont.)	Outline (cont.)
	B. The Marks of Mature Believers, 1:3-11	bonds, and in the defence and confirmation of the gospel, ye all are partakers of my grace.	c. Partners in the gospel d. Partners in grace e. Partners with Christ
1. The mark of a thankful heart	3 I thank my God upon every remembrance of you,	8 For God is my record, how greatly I long after you all in the bowels of Jesus Christ.	
2. The mark of prayer **3. The mark of joy**	4 Always in every prayer of mine for you all making request with joy,	9 And this I pray, that your love may abound yet more and more in knowledge and in all judgment;	**7. The mark of a growing & discerning love**
4. The mark of fellowship	5 For your fellowship in the gospel from the first day until now;		
5. The mark of confidence in God's salvation a. Is a good work b. Is incomplete c. Is to be completed at Christ's return	6 Being confident of this very thing, that he which hath begun a good work in you will perform it until the day of Jesus Christ:	10 That ye may approve things that are excellent; that ye may be sincere and without offence till the day of Christ;	a. To approve the excellent b. To live pure lives c. To cause no one to stumble
6. The mark of partnership a. Partners in heart b. Partners in suffering	7 Even as it is meet for me to think this of you all, because I have you in my heart; inasmuch as both in my	11 Being filled with the fruits of righteousness, which are by Jesus Christ, unto the glory and praise of God.	**8. The mark of righteousness**

Section I
THE MARKS OF GOD'S PEOPLE, Philippians 1:1-30

Study 2: THE MARKS OF MATURE BELIEVERS

Text: Philippians 1:3-11

Aim: To honestly measure your own spiritual maturity.

Memory Verse:
"Being confident of this very thing, that He which hath begun a good work in you will perform it until the day of Jesus Christ" (Ph.1:6).

INTRODUCTION:
What are the marks of a mature Christian believer? What are the marks of a dynamic, mature Christian church? This passage answers these questions. Concisely and clearly, the marks so desperately needed by believers and churches are spelled out.

OUTLINE:
1. The mark of a thankful heart (v.3).
2. The mark of prayer (v.4).
3. The mark of joy (v.4).
4. The mark of fellowship (v.5).
5. The mark of confidence in God's salvation (v.6).
6. The mark of partnership (v.7-8).
7. The mark of a growing and discerning love (v.9-10).
8. The mark of righteousness (v.11).

PHILIPPIANS 1:3-11

PERSONAL OUTLINE NOTES

1. THE FIRST MEASURING MARK: A THANKFUL HEART (v.3).

2. THE SECOND MEASURING MARK: PRAYER (v.4).

3. THE THIRD MEASURING MARK: JOY (v.4).

PERSONAL OUTLINE NOTES (continued)

4. THE FOURTH MEASURING MARK: FELLOWSHIP (v.5).

5. THE FIFTH MEASURING MARK: AN UNSHAKEN CONFIDENCE IN GOD'S SALVATION (v.6).

6. THE SIXTH MEASURING MARK: PARTNERSHIP (v.7-8).

PERSONAL OUTLINE NOTES (continued)

7. THE SEVENTH MEASURING MARK: A GROWING AND DISCERNING LOVE (v.9-10).

8. THE EIGHTH MEASURING MARK: RIGHTEOUSNESS (v.11).

SUMMARY:

Every Christian believer can measure his spiritual maturity by looking at these marks within his life. Are these marks in your life?

1. A thankful heart
2. A consistent prayer life
3. A heart and life full of joy
4. A strong fellowship with other believers
5. An unshaken confidence in God's salvation
6. A partnership with other Christian believers
7. A growing and discerning love
8. A life of righteousness

PHILIPPIANS 1:3-11

PERSONAL JOURNAL NOTES
(Reflection & Response)

1. The most important thing that I learned from this lesson was:

2. The area that I need to work on the most is:

3. I can apply this lesson to my life by:

4. Closing statement of commitment:

PHILIPPIANS 1:3-11

ADDITIONAL NOTES

C. The Marks of a Mature & Active Witness, 1:12-19

12 But I would ye
should understand breth-
ren, that the things
which happened unto
me have fallen out
rather unto the fur-
therance of the gospel;
13 So that my bonds
in Christ are manifest
in all the palace, and
in all other places;
14 And many of the
brethren in the Lord,
waxing confident by
my bonds, are much
more bold to speak
the word without
fear.
15 Some indeed preach
Christ even of envy
and strife, and some
also of good will:
16 The one preach
Christ of contention,
not sincerely, sup-
posing to add afflic-
tion to my bonds:
17 But the other of
love, knowing that I
am set for the defence
of the gospel.
18 What then? not-
withstanding, every
way, whether in pre-
tence, or in truth,
Christ is preached; and
I therein do rejoice,
yea, and will rejoice.
19 For I know that
this shall turn to my
salvation through your
prayer, and the supply
of the Spirit of Jesus
Christ,

1. **He shares the gospel regardless of circumstances**
   a. Paul faced dark circumstances: He was a prisoner in Rome
   b. Paul used his dark circumstances to spread the gospel
      1) Spread through the elite guard of Rome: In the palace & everywhere else
      2) Spread by encouraging believers to be more fearless witnesses
2. **He holds no personal jealousy nor desire for credit or prestige**
   a. Others preached Christ with jealous & contentious spirits, hoping to cause trouble for Paul
   b. Still others preached in love, supporting Paul
   c. Paul rejoiced in this one thing: Christ was being preached--whether from false motives or true, Christ was preached
3. **He possesses the assurance of a happy ending: Salvation**
   a. Through prayer
   b. Through the Holy Spirit

Section I
THE MARKS OF GOD'S PEOPLE, Phillipians 1:1-30

Study 3: **THE MARKS OF A MATURE WITNESS**

Text: **Philippians 1:12-19**

Aim: To become a mature and active witness for Christ.

Memory Verse:

"For we cannot but speak the things which we have seen and heard" (Acts 4:20).

INTRODUCTION:

Circumstances often throw and defeat people. The maturity of a person can be seen by how well he handles the things that happen to him--the things that affect a person with mood changes ranging from mild to severe. The one thing that a believer must do is to learn to live above circumstances--to keep his witness for Christ strong and mature. This is the subject of the present passage: the marks of a mature witness.

OUTLINE:

1. He shares the gospel regardless of circumstances (v.12-14).
2. He holds no personal jealousy nor desire for credit or prestige (v.15-18).
3. He possesses the assurance of a happy ending: salvation (v.19).

PHILIPPIANS 1:12-19

PERSONAL OUTLINE NOTES

1. A MATURE WITNESS SHARES THE GOSPEL REGARDLESS OF THE CIRCUMSTANCES (V.12-14).

2. A MATURE WITNESS HOLDS NO PERSONAL JEALOUSY NOR DESIRE FOR CREDIT OR PRESTIGE (v.15-18).

3. A MATURE WITNESS POSSESSES THE ASSURANCE OF A HAPPY ENDING: SALVATION (v.19).

PHILIPPIANS 1:12-19

SUMMARY:

God expects you to become a mature witness for Him. God expects you to:

1. Share the gospel, regardless of circumstances
2. Hold no personal desire for credit or glory
3. Be assured of a happy ending, that of salvation

PERSONAL JOURNAL NOTES
(Reflection & Response)

1. The most important thing that I learned from this lesson was:

2. The area that I need to work on the most is:

3. I can apply this lesson to my life by:

4. Closing statement of commitment:

PHILIPPIANS 1:12-19

ADDITIONAL NOTES

	D. The Marks of the Great Christian Believer, 1:20-26	I shall choose I wot not. 23 For I am in a strait betwixt two, having a	
1. One great expectation & hope: To magnify Christ in his body	20 According to my earnest expectation and my hope, that in nothing I shall be ashamed, but that with all boldness, as always, so now also Christ shall be magnified in my body, whether it be by life, or by death.	desire to depart, and to be with Christ; which is far better: 24 Nevertheless to abide in the flesh is more needful for you. 25 And having this confidence, I know that I shall abide and continue with you all for your furtherance	**4. One great willingness: To serve sacrificially** a. By proclaiming the believer's faith
2. One great commitment in life & death: Christ	21 For to me to live is Christ, and to die is gain.	and joy of faith; 26 That your rejoicing may be more abundant	
3. One great dilemma: Whether To live or to depart to be with Christ	22 But if I live in the flesh, this is the fruit of my labour: yet what	in Jesus Christ for me by my coming to you again.	b. By fellowshipping with believers

Section I
THE MARKS OF GOD'S PEOPLE, Philippians 1:1-30

Study 4: **THE MARKS OF THE GREAT CHRISTIAN BELIEVER**

Text: **Philippians 1:20-26**

Aim: To firmly adopt the marks of a great Christian believer.

Memory Verse:
"For to me to live is Christ, and to die is gain" (Philippians 1:21).

INTRODUCTION:

If a man has ever lived a life of commitment to our Lord Jesus Christ, it was Paul. Remember, he was in prison facing a capital crime with his deliverance looking almost hopeless. Death was staring him in the face. This passage is one of the great passages of Scripture. Verse 21 has been adopted by many believers as their life verse. Many have committed their lives to pursue either verse twenty or twenty-one. This is the personal testimony of Paul: the marks of the great Christian believer: a life of commitment.

OUTLINE:

1. There is one great expectation and hope: to magnify Christ in one's body (v.20).
2. There is one great commitment in life and death: Christ (v.21).
3. There is one great dilemma: whether to live or to depart to be with Christ (v.22-23).
4. There is one great willingness: to serve sacrificially (v.24-26).

PHILIPPIANS 1:20-26

PERSONAL OUTLINE NOTES

1. **ONE GREAT EXPECTATION & HOPE: TO MAGNIFY CHRIST IN YOUR BODY (v.20).**

2. **ONE GREAT COMMITMENT IN LIFE & DEATH: CHRIST (v.21).**

3. **ONE GREAT DILEMMA: WHETHER TO LIVE OR TO DEPART TO BE WITH CHRIST (v.22,23).**

PERSONAL OUTLINE NOTES (continued)

4. ONE GREAT WILLINGNESS: TO SERVE SACRIFICIALLY (v.24-26).

SUMMARY:

God has called every believer to be a great Christian, including you. God wants you to have...

1. One great expectation and hope: to magnify Christ in your body.
2. One great commitment in life and death: Christ.
3. One great dilemma: whether to live or to depart to be with Christ.
4. One great willingness: to serve sacrificially.

PHILIPPIANS 1:20-26

PERSONAL JOURNAL NOTES
(Reflection & Response)

1. The most important thing that I learned from this lesson was:

2. The area that I need to work on the most is:

3. I can apply this lesson to my life by:

4. Closing statement of commitment:

PHILIPPIANS 1:27-30

	E. The Marks of the Great Christian Church, 1:27-30	28 And in nothing terrified by your adversaries: which is to them an evident token of perdition, but to you of salvation, and that of God.	**4. Mark 4: Courage & fearlessness** a. Persecution is a sign of destruction b. Persecution is a sign of salvation
1. Mark 1: Christian conduct—heavenly citizenship **2. Mark 2: Honoring the gospel** **3. Mark 3: Standing fast** a. Must stand fast in one spirit & with one mind b. Must stand fast in striving together for the faith of the gospel	27 Only let your conversation be as it becometh the gospel of Christ: that whether I come and see you, or else be absent, I may hear of your affairs, that ye stand fast in one spirit, with one mind striving together for the faith of the gospel.	29 For unto you it is given in the behalf of Christ, not only to believe on him, but also to suffer for his sake; 30 Having the same conflict which ye saw in me, and now hear to be in me.	c. Persecution is a privilege d. Paul left a dynamic example in bearing persecution

Section I
THE MARKS OF GOD'S PEOPLE, Philippians 1:1-30

Study 5: THE MARKS OF THE GREAT CHRISTIAN CHURCH

Text: Philippians 1:27-30

Aim: To make a serious commitment to build a great Christian church.

Memory Verse:

"For unto you it is given in the behalf of Christ, not only to believe on Him, but also to suffer for His sake" (Philippians 1:29).

INTRODUCTION:

Paul was in prison. He faced a capital crime, and there was a strong chance he might be executed. He did not think so, but there was a possibility. He was not sure if he would ever see the Philippian church again, so he sat down and began to write to them. What would you say if you were writing to a group of God's people for the last time? One of the subjects that concerned Paul was the subject of this passage: the marks of a great church. The Philippian church was a great church, and Paul wanted it to remain great. Therefore, he reviewed with them the marks of a great Christian church.

OUTLINE:

1. Mark 1: Christian conduct—heavenly citizenship (v.27).
2. Mark 2: honoring the gospel (v.27).
3. Mark 3: standing fast (v.27).
4. Mark 4: courage and fearlessness (v.28-30).

PHILIPPIANS 1:27-30

PERSONAL OUTLINE NOTES

1. MARK 1: CHRISTIAN CONDUCT—HEAVENLY CITIZENSHIP (v.27).

2. MARK 2: HONORING THE GOSPEL (v.27).

3. MARK 3: STANDING FAST (v.27).

PERSONAL OUTLINE NOTES (continued)

4. MARK 4: COURAGE & FEARLESSNESS (v.28-30).

SUMMARY:

A church is great when it is structured like a Great Commission Church. When that is true, the following four marks are evident:
Mark 1: Christian conduct—heavenly citizenship
Mark 2: Honoring the gospel
Mark 3: Standing fast
Mark 4: Courage & fearlessness

How does your church measure up? What is your part in its success as a Great Commission Church?

PHILIPPIANS 1:27-30

PERSONAL JOURNAL NOTES
(Reflection & Response)

1. The most important thing that I learned from this lesson was:

2. The area that I need to work on the most is:

3. I can apply this lesson to my life by:

4. Closing statement of commitment:

	CHAPTER 2 II. THE STEPS TO UNITY, 2:1-18 A. Christ--The Traits of His Life in Us, 2:1-4	2 Fulfil ye my joy, that ye be likeminded, having the same love, being of one accord, of one mind.	**5. The trait of concern for one another's joy**
		3 Let nothing be done through strife or vainglory; but in lowliness of mind let each	**6. The trait of humility or lowliness of mind**
1. The trait of consolation	If there be therefore any consolation in	esteem other better than themselves.	
2. The trait of love **3. The trait of fellowship in the Spirit** **4. The trait of compassion**	Christ, if any comfort of love, if any fellowship of the Spirit, if any bowels and mercies	4 Look not every man on his own things, but every man also on the things of others.	**7. The trait of controlling self-interest or concentration upon oneself**

Section II
THE STEPS TO UNITY, Philippians 2:1-18

Study 1: CHRIST—THE TRAITS OF HIS LIFE IN US

Text: Philippians 2:1-4

Aim: To embrace the character traits of Christ: To become more like Him.

Memory Verse:

"Let nothing be done through strife or vainglory; but in lowliness of mind let each esteem other better than themselves" (Philippians 2:3).

INTRODUCTION:

The Philippian church was a very strong church. When a church is strong, it is always full of vision and planning, and it is always working out a strategy to carry forth the gospel. A strong church launches ministry after ministry and program after program. It is never still and never complacent—neither the minds of the people nor the hands of the people. Because of this, there is always the danger of differences of opinion: differences in vision, desires, concern, emphasis, and interest. There are always different ideas as to which ministry or project should be undertaken and supported and a host of other differences.

The point is this: the more strength and activity a church has, the more attention it must give to unity. Why? Because a strong church has more minds and bodies working, and where more people are working more differences are bound to arise. Consequently, the members must give more attention to unity.

Paul knew this; he knew that he had to put the Philippian church on guard. The church had to protect itself against disunity and division. This is the subject of chapter two: The Steps to Unity (2:1-18).

The first step to unity is Christ—allowing His life to be lived out in us. In particular there are seven traits that will hold the church together and keep it unified.

OUTLINE:

1. The trait of consolation (v.1).
2. The trait of love (v.1).
3. The trait of fellowship in the Spirit (v.1).
4. The trait of compassion (v.1).
5. The trait of concern for one another's joy (v.2).
6. The trait of humility or lowliness of mind (v.3).
7. The trait of controlling self-interest or concentration upon oneself (v.4).

PHILIPPIANS 2:1-4

PERSONAL OUTLINE NOTES

1. THE TRAIT OF CONSOLATION (v.1).

2. THE TRAIT OF LOVE (v.1).

3. THE TRAIT OF FELLOWSHIP IN THE SPIRIT (v.1).

PHILIPPIANS 2:1-4

PERSONAL OUTLINE NOTES (continued)

4. THE TRAIT OF COMPASSION (v.1).

5. THE TRAIT OF CONCERN FOR ONE ANOTHER'S JOY (v.2).

6. THE TRAIT OF HUMILITY OR LOWLINESS OF MIND (v.3).

PERSONAL OUTLINE NOTES (continued)

7. THE TRAIT OF CONTROLLING SELF-INTEREST OR CONCENTRATION UPON YOURSELF (v.4).

SUMMARY:

Do you want to be a part of a church that learns to walk in His steps? If so, a Christian church can be a place of unity if the following traits are applied:

1. The trait of consolation
2. The trait of love
3. The trait of fellowship in the Spirit
4. The trait of compassion
5. The trait of concern for one another's joy
6. The trait of humility or lowliness of mind
7. The trait of controlling self-interest or concentration upon oneself

Let these traits become the possession of a group of Christians, and the lost will long to be with you.

PHILIPPIANS 2:1-4

PERSONAL JOURNAL NOTES
(Reflection & Response)

1. The most important thing that I learned from this lesson was:

2. The area that I need to work on the most is:

3. I can apply this lesson to my life by:

4. Closing statement of commitment:

PHILIPPIANS 2:1-4

ADDITIONAL NOTES

PHILIPPIANS 2:5-11

	B. Humbling One's Self, 2:5-11	became obedient unto death, even the death of the cross.	**to the very point of death**
1. Christ is the supreme example	5 Let this mind be in you, which was also in Christ Jesus:	9 Wherefore God also hath highly exalted him, and given him a	**5. Christ was rewarded—highly exalted by God**
2. Christ is of the very nature of God	6 Who, being in the form of God, thought it not robbery to be equal with God:	name which is above every name: 10 That at the name of Jesus every knee	a. Given a name above every name b. Given supreme power & authority
3. Christ emptied Himself & became a man	7 But made himself of no reputation, and took upon him the form of a servant, and was made in the likeness of men:	should bow, of things in heaven, and things in earth, and things under the earth; 11 And that every tongue should confess	c. Given supreme worship as Lord
4. Christ humbled Himself to the point of utter humiliation--	8 And being found in fashion as a man, he humbled himself, and	that Jesus Christ is Lord, to the glory of God the Father.	

Section II
THE STEPS TO UNITY, Philippians 2:1-18

Study 2: HUMBLING ONE'S SELF

Text: Philippians 2:5-11

Aim: To learn a much needed lesson: How to let the humility of Christ flow through you.

Memory Verse:
"Let this mind be in you, which was also in Christ Jesus" (Philippians 2:5).

INTRODUCTION:
This is one of the greatest passages ever written about Jesus Christ. It paints the perfect picture of humility—the humility of Jesus Christ. No one has ever come close to humbling himself like Jesus Christ did, and no one ever will. Yet, if the problems of the church and of the world are to ever be solved, we must humble ourselves just as Christ did. The church is too often divided, too often rumbling with criticism, murmuring, differences, jealousy, envy, ambition, outside talk, negative feelings, and desires for position and recognition. The only answer is the declaration of this passage: letting the humility of Jesus Christ flow in and out of our minds. The first step to unity is letting Christ live in us. Humility is the second step to unity. The unity of a church depends upon its members walking in the humility of Jesus Christ.

OUTLINE:
1. Christ is the supreme example (v.5).
2. Christ is of the very nature of God (v.6).
3. Christ emptied Himself and became a man (v.7).
4. Christ humbled Himself to the point of utter humiliation—to the very point of death (v.8).
5. Christ was rewarded—highly exalted by God (v.9-11).

PHILIPPIANS 2:5-11

PERSONAL OUTLINE NOTES

1. CHRIST IS THE SUPREME EXAMPLE (v.5).

2. CHRIST IS THE VERY NATURE OF GOD (v.6).

3. CHRIST EMPTIED HIMSELF & BECAME A MAN (v.7).

PERSONAL OUTLINE NOTES (continued)

4. CHRIST HUMBLED HIMSELF TO THE POINT OF UTTER HUMILIATION—TO THE VERY POINT OF DEATH (v.8).

5. CHRIST WAS REWARDED—HIGHLY EXALTED BY GOD (v.9-11).

SUMMARY:

Christ's example of humility is a lofty one indeed. In fact, it is impossible to attain unless He fills you with His Holy Spirit every day.

A review of the lesson will remind you that:

1. Christ is the supreme example
2. Christ is the very nature of God
3. Christ emptied Himself & became a man
4. Christ humbled Himself to the point of utter humiliation—to the very point of death
5. Christ was rewarded—highly exalted by God

PHILIPPIANS 2:5-11

PERSONAL JOURNAL NOTES
(Reflection & Response)

1. The most important thing that I learned from this lesson was:

2. The area that I need to work on the most is:

3. I can apply this lesson to my life by:

4. Closing statement of commitment:

	C. Working Out One's Own Salvation or Deliverance, 2:12-18	blameless and harmless, the sons of God, without rebuke, in the midst of a crooked and perverse nation,	**work at being pure** a. Blameless b. Harmless, sincere c. Without rebuke
1. The first work: To work out one's own salvation (deliverance) with fear & trembling	12 Wherefore, my beloved, as ye have always obeyed, not as in my presence only, but now much more in my absence, work out your own salvation with fear and trembling.	among whom ye shine as lights in the world; 16 Holding forth the word of life; that I may rejoice in the day of Christ, that I have not run in vain, neither laboured in vain.	**5. The fifth work: To work at witnessing**
2. The second work: To work at obedience–to work out God's stirrings within the heart	13 For it is God which worketh in you both to will and to do of his good pleasure.	17 Yea, and if I be offered upon the sacrifice and service of your faith, I joy, and rejoice with you all.	**6. The sixth work: To work at following the example of sacrificial labor**
3. The third work: To work at not murmuring	14 Do all things without murmurings and disputings:	18 For the same cause also do ye joy, and	
4. The fourth work: To	15 That ye may be	rejoice with me.	

Section II
THE STEPS TO UNITY, Philippians 2:1-18

Study 3: WORKING OUT ONE'S OWN SALVATION OR DELIVERANCE

Text: **Philippians 2:12-18**

Aim: To learn the practical duties of the Christian life: What you need to do *after* you have been saved.

Memory Verse:
"For it is God which worketh in you both to will and to do of His good pleasure"(Philippians 2:13).

INTRODUCTION:

This passage is still dealing with unity—unity in the church and unity among believers. But the passage is unique because it brings up the great subject of salvation. Keep in mind that salvation means deliverance and that salvation is of God. It is God who has saved and delivered you: "For by grace are ye saved" (Eph.2:8-9). But once you are saved, go to work—work out your own salvation and deliverance. Salvation is not stagnant and complacent. A saved person is not to be sitting around doing nothing and letting the chips fall where they may. A saved person is to get up and go to work. He is to do all he can to work out his own deliverance. This is the subject of the present passage. If the church is to be unified—if believers are to walk in a spirit of unity, then they must look at their salvation—at the whole scope of their lives and the glorious salvation God has given them—and they must do all they can to work out their own deliverance.

OUTLINE:

1. The first work: to work out one's own salvation (deliverance) with fear and trembling (v.12).
2. The second work: to work at obedience—to work out the stirrings of God within the heart (v.13).
3. The third work: to work at not murmuring (v.14).
4. The fourth work: to work at being pure (v.15).
5. The fifth work: to work at witnessing (v.16).
6. The sixth work: to work at following the example of sacrificial labor (v.17-18).

PHILIPPIANS 2:12-18

PERSONAL OUTLINE NOTES

1. **THE FIRST WORK: TO WORK OUT ONE'S SALVATION (DELIVERANCE) WITH FEAR AND TREMBLING (VS 12).**

2. **THE SECOND WORK: TO WORK AT OBEDIENCE—TO WORK OUT GOD'S STIRRINGS WITHIN THE HEART (v.13).**

3. **THE THIRD WORK: TO WORK AT NOT MURMURING (v.14).**

<u>PERSONAL OUTLINE NOTES</u> (continued)

4. THE FOURTH WORK: TO WORK AT BEING PURE (V.15).

5. THE FIFTH WORK: TO WORK AT WITNESSING (v.16).

6. THE SIXTH WORK: TO WORK AT FOLLOWING THE EXAMPLE OF SACRIFICIAL LABOR (v.17-18).

PHILIPPIANS 2:12-18

SUMMARY:

As you work out your salvation, remember that the Christian has six items of work to do:

1. Work out your own salvation with fear and trembling
2. Work at obedience
3. Work at not murmuring
4. Work at being pure
5. Work at witnessing
6. Work at following the example of sacrificial labor

PERSONAL JOURNAL NOTES
(Reflection & Response)

1. The most important thing that I learned from this lesson was:

2. The area that I need to work on the most is:

3. I can apply this lesson to my life by:

4. Closing statement of commitment:

	III. THE EXAMPLES OF SOME CHRISTIAN BELIEVERS, 2:19-30	20 For I have no man likeminded, who will naturally care for your state.	**2. He had a kindred, brotherly spirit in caring for others**
	A. The Example of Timothy--a Young Man Who Willingly Served In Second Place, 2:19-24	21 For all seek their own, not the things which are Jesus Christ's.	**3. He was willing to deny himself--to be obsessed with the things of Christ**
		22 But ye know the proof of him, that, as a son with the father, he hath served with me in the gospel.	**4. He was willing to be a son, a disciple** a. Willing to be tried & proven
1. Timothy--a young man who willingly served in second place	19 But I trust in the Lord Jesus to send Timothe-us shortly unto you, that I also may be of good comfort, when I know your state.	23 Him therefore I hope to send presently, so soon as I shall see how it will go with me. 24 But I trust in the Lord that I also myself shall come shortly.	b. Willing to go as sent

Section III
THE EXAMPLES OF SOME CHRISTIAN BELIEVERS, Philippians 2:19-30

Study 1: THE EXAMPLE OF TIMOTHY—A YOUNG MAN WHO WILLINGLY SERVED IN SECOND PLACE

Text: **Philippians 2:19-24**

Aim: To make a permanent decision to serve wherever God calls you.

Memory Verse:

"Not that I speak in respect of want: for I have learned, in whatsoever state I am, therewith to be content" (Philippians 4:11).

INTRODUCTION:

Nothing challenges the human heart any more than the faithful example of others. This passage gives us the dynamic example of a man who was totally committed to Jesus Christ: Timothy. Timothy was a young man who willingly served in second place.

OUTLINE:

1. Timothy—a young man who willingly served in second place (v.19).
2. He had a kindred, brotherly spirit in caring for others (v.20).
3. He was willing to deny himself—to be obsessed with the things of Christ (v.21).
4. He was willing to be a son, a disciple (v.22-24).

PHILIPPIANS 2:19-24

PERSONAL OUTLINE NOTES

1. TIMOTHY, A YOUNG MAN WHO WILLINGLY SERVED IN SECOND PLACE (v.19).

2. HE HAD A KINDRED, BROTHERLY SPIRIT IN CARING FOR OTHERS (v.20).

3. HE WAS WILLING TO DENY HIMSELF—TO BE OBSESSED WITH THE THINGS OF CHRIST (v.21).

PERSONAL OUTLINE NOTES (continued)

4. HE WAS WILLING TO BE A SON, A DISCIPLE (v.22-24).

SUMMARY:

You have observed the qualities that Timothy had in serving as "number two." In review, they are:

1. Timothy was a young man who willingly served in second place.
2. He had a kindred, brotherly spirit in caring for others.
3. He was willing to deny himself—to be obsessed with the things of Christ.
4. He was willing to be a son, a disciple.

Timothy was *willing*...are you?

PHILIPPIANS 2:19-24

PERSONAL JOURNAL NOTES
(Reflection & Response)

1. The most important thing that I learned from this lesson was:

2. The area that I need to work on the most is:

3. I can apply this lesson to my life by:

4. Closing statement of commitment:

	B. The Example of Epaphroditus--a Man Who Was Not a Quitter Nor a Coward, 2:25-30	sick nigh unto death: but God had mercy on him; and not on him only, but on me also, lest I should have sorrow upon sorrow.	**forsake God**
1. He did not quit nor forsake his brother	25 Yet I supposed it necessary to send to you Epaphroditus, my brother, and companion in labour, and fellowsoldier, but your messenger, and he that ministered to my wants.	28 I sent him therefore the more carefully, that, when ye see him again, ye may rejoice, and that I may be the less sorrowful.	**4. Conclusion: The appeal** a. Paul is sending him back to the church so the church can joy & rejoice in him
		29 Receive him therefore in the Lord with all gladness; and hold such in reputation:	b. Receive him: He builds his reputation; he gambles & risks his life for Christ
2. He did not quit nor forsake the church	26 For he longed after you all, and was full of heaviness, because that ye had heard that he had been sick.	30 Because for the work of Christ he was nigh unto death, not regarding his life, to supply your lack of service toward me.	
3. He did not quit nor	27 For indeed he was		

Section III
THE EXAMPLES OF SOME CHRISTIAN BELIEVERS,
Philippians 2:19-30

Study 2: THE EXAMPLE OF EPAPHRODITUS—A MAN WHO WAS NOT A QUITTER NOR A COWARD

Text: Philippians 2:25-30

Aim: To make one great promise to Christ: To never quit.

Memory Verse:

> **"Therefore, my beloved brethren, be ye stedfast, unmoveable, always abounding in the work of the Lord, forasmuch as ye know that your labour is not in vain in the Lord (1 Cor.15:58).**

INTRODUCTION:

The Philippian church had heard that Paul was in prison and that he was having an extremely difficult time. Their hearts went out to him, so they decided to do two things: to take up an offering to meet Paul's material needs and to send a dedicated layman who could remain with him to help him. Such a man would have to be savagely brave, for by attaching himself to a man facing a capital crime, he would be leaving himself open to the charge of being an accomplice. By helping Paul, the man would be risking his own life. The man chosen was Epaphroditus.

While in Rome, Epaphroditus fell seriously ill and came close to death. News of his illness reached Philippi. And in turn, news returned to Epaphroditus that his home church was worried over his welfare. He in turn began to worry over them. But God spared him; and after gaining his strength, Paul felt for some reason (perhaps to keep this illness from recurring or to eliminate the possibility of his being arrested) that Epaphroditus should return to Philippi.

But the possibility of a problem existed. If he returned before Paul's fate was known, some would call him a quitter, a coward, a failure.[1] The answer to this criticism is the very reason for this passage. Paul gives a glowing appraisal of their messenger.

PHILIPPIANS 2:25-30

OUTLINE:

1. He did not quit nor forsake his brother (v.25).
2. He did not quit nor forsake the church (v.26).
3. He did not quit nor forsake God (v.27).
4. Conclusion: the appeal to joy and to receive the person who is not a quitter (v.28-30).

PERSONAL OUTLINE NOTES

1. HE DID NOT QUIT NOR FORSAKE HIS BROTHER (v.25).

2. HE DID NOT QUIT NOR FORSAKE THE CHURCH (v.26).

3. HE DID NOT QUIT NOR FORSAKE GOD (v.27).

PERSONAL OUTLINE NOTES (continued)

4. CONCLUSION: THE APPEAL TO JOY AND TO RECEIVE THE PERSON WHO IS NOT A QUITTER (v.28-30).

SUMMARY:

You have seen the testimony of a man whose courage is an example for every believer to follow. He never, never, never gave up. Like Epaphroditus…

1. You must learn to never quit nor forsake your Christian brothers and sisters in Christ.
2. You must learn to never quit nor forsake the church.
3. You must learn never to quit nor forsake God.
4. Result: If you never quit, then other believers will joy and receive you.

PHILIPPIANS 2:25-30

PERSONAL JOURNAL NOTES
(Reflection & Response)

1. The most important thing that I learned from this lesson was:

2. The area that I need to work on the most is:

3. I can apply this lesson to my life by:

4. Closing statement of commitment:

---

[1]William Barclay, *The Letters to the Philippians, Colossians, and Thessalonians*, p.60f.

	CHAPTER 3 IV. THE "PRESSING ON" OF THE CHRISTIAN BELIEVER, 3:1-21 A. Pressing On: Guarding Oneself, 3:1-3	write the same things to you, to me indeed is not grievous, but for you it is safe.	2. By heeding what is written (the Scripture)
		2 Beware of dogs, beware of evil workers, beware of the concision.	3. By watching out for false teachers
		3 For we are the circumcision, which worship God in the spirit, and rejoice in Christ Jesus, and have no confidence in the flesh.	4. By knowing that you are the true (spiritual) circumcision, a true believer
1. By rejoicing in the Lord	Finally, my brethren, rejoice in the Lord. To		

Section IV
THE "PRESSING ON" OF THE CHRISTIAN BELIEVER, Philippians 3:1-21

Study 1: PRESSING ON—GUARDING ONESELF

Text: Philippians 3:1-3

Aim: To learn how to constantly guard your Christian life.

Memory Verse:

"For we are the circumcision [true believers], which worship God in the spirit, and rejoice in Christ Jesus, and have no confidence in the flesh"(Philippians 3:3).

INTRODUCTION:

This chapter is one of the great chapters of the Bible, a chapter that needs to be studied time and again. It includes the great personal testimony and ambition of Paul. It gives us some of the great principles that governed Paul's life. The subject of the chapter is "The Pressing On Of The Christian Believer." These are some things the Christian believer must do as he presses on for Christ. First, he must guard himself.

OUTLINE:

1. By rejoicing in the Lord (v.1).
2. By heeding what is written (the Scripture) (v.1).
3. By watching out for false teachers (v.2).
4. By knowing that you are the true (spiritual) circumcision, a true believer (v.3).

PHILIPPIANS 3:1-3

PERSONAL OUTLINE NOTES

1. BY REJOICING IN THE LORD (v.1).

2. BY HEEDING WHAT IS WRITTEN (THE SCRIPTURE) (v.1).

3. BY WATCHING OUT FOR FALSE TEACHERS (v.2).

PERSONAL OUTLINE NOTES (continued)

4. BY KNOWING THAT YOU ARE THE TRUE [SPIRITUAL] CIRCUMCISION, A TRUE BELIEVER (v.3).

SUMMARY:

You must press on and guard yourself by:

1. Rejoicing in the Lord, staying in His presence always.
2. Heeding what is written in Scripture and being obedient.
3. Watching out for false teachers.
4. Knowing that you are the 'true circumcision,' a true believer.

PHILIPPIANS 3:1-3

PERSONAL JOURNAL NOTES
(Reflection & Response)

1. The most important thing that I learned from this lesson was:

2. The area that I need to work on the most is:

3. I can apply this lesson to my life by:

4. Closing statement of commitment:

Outline	Scripture
	B. Pressing on: Paul's Personal Testimony--Rejecting Self-righteousness & Seeking Perfection, 3:4-16
1. Paul had achieved the height of self-righteousness, but he rejected it	4 Though I might also have confidence in the flesh. If any other man thinketh that he hath whereof he might trust in the flesh, I more:
a. He had the right parents b. He had the heritage c. He had the social status d. He had the faithfulness	5 Circumcised the eighth day, of the stock of Israel, of the tribe of Benjamin, an Hebrew of the Hebrews; as touching the law, a Pharisee;
e. He had the religion f. He had the religious zeal g. He had the morality	6 Concerning zeal, persecuting the church; touching the righteousness which is in the law, blameless.
2. Paul sought to win Christ--His righteousness, His perfection	7 But what things were gain to me, those I counted loss for Christ.
a. Paul had a past experience with Christ: He had counted his own righteousness as loss b. Paul had a continuous experience with Christ: He counted all things as waste	8 Yea doubtless, and I count all things but loss for the excellency of the knowledge of Christ Jesus my Lord: for whom I have suffered the loss of all things, and do count them but dung, that I may win Christ,
c. Paul sought a future exerience with Christ: to be found in Christ	9 And be found in him, not having mine own righteousness, which is of the law, but that which is through the faith of by faith: Christ, the righteousness which is of God
d. Paul sought a victorious experience with Christ: To know His glorious power over the world & over all that is in the world	10 That I may know him, and the power of his resurrection, and the fellowship of his sufferings, being made conformable unto his death;
e. Paul sought an eternal experience with Christ: To be resurrected from the dead	11 If by any means I might attain unto the resurrection of the dead.
3. Paul did not count himself as having yet arrived--he was not yet perfect a. He followed after his God-given purpose	12 Not as though I had already attained, either were already perfect: but I follow after, if that I may apprehend that for which also I am apprehended of Christ Jesus.
b. He worked at forgetting the past	13 Brethren, I count not myself to have apprehended: but this one thing I do, forgetting those things which are behind, and reaching forth unto those things which are before,
c. He pressed on toward the goal, toward God's purpose in Christ Jesus	14 I press toward the mark for the prize of the high calling of God in Christ Jesus.
d. He kept his mind on growing, on maturing in Christ	15 Let us therefore, as many as be perfect, be thus minded: and if in any thing ye be otherwise minded, God shall reveal even this unto you.
e. He maintained the growth he had already achieved	16 Nevertheless, whereto we have already attained, let us walk by the same rule, let us mind the same thing.

Section IV
THE 'PRESSING ON' OF THE CHRISTIAN BELIEVER, Philippians 3:1-21

(Note: Because of the length of this outline and commentary, you may wish to split this passage into two or three studies.)

PHILIPPIANS 3:4-16

Study 2: PRESSING ON: PAUL'S PERSONAL TESTIMONY—REJECTING SELF-RIGHTEOUSNESS & SEEKING PERFECTION

Text: Philippians 3:4-16

Aim: To reject self-righteousness and pursue the righteousness of Christ.

Memory Verse:
"I press toward the mark for the prize of the high calling of God in Christ Jesus" (Philippians 3:14).

INTRODUCTION

Paul had never seen the great love of God for man. Yet, *above all men*, he had given his life to seeking after God, doing all the good he could to make himself acceptable to God. But despite all his achievements, he still did not have peace with God. Perfect assurance and confidence of living eternally with God was still lacking. This is the message of the present passage: Paul's personal testimony—his rejection of self-righteousness and turning to the righteousness of Jesus Christ.

OUTLINE:

1. Paul had achieved the height of self-righteousness, but he rejected it (v.4-6).
2. Paul sought to win Christ—His righteousness and perfection (v.7-11).
3. Paul did not count himself as having yet arrived—he was not yet perfect (v.12-16).

PHILIPPIANS 3:4-16

PERSONAL OUTLINE NOTES

1. PAUL HAD ACHIEVED THE HEIGHT OF SELF-RIGHTEOUSNESS, BUT HE REJECTED IT (v.4-6).

PERSONAL OUTLINE NOTES (continued)

2. PAUL SOUGHT TO WIN CHRIST—HIS RIGHTEOUSNES, HIS PERFECTION (v.7-11).

PERSONAL OUTLINE NOTES (continued)

3. PAUL DID NOT COUNT HIMSELF AS HAVING YET ARRIVED—HE WAS NOT YET PERFECT (v.12-16).

PHILIPPIANS 3:4-16

SUMMARY:

You have learned how Paul attempted to know God and have seen ways to apply these lessons to your own life.

1. You must reject self-righteousness.
2. You must seek to win Christ—His righteousness, His perfection.
3. You must not count yourself as having yet arrived—you are not yet perfect.

PERSONAL JOURNAL NOTES
(Reflection & Response)

1. The most important thing that I learned from this lesson was:

2. The area that I need to work on the most is:

3. I can apply this lesson to my life by:

4. Closing statement of commitment:

1. Reason 1: Some walk as good examples a. Paul walked as an example b. Others walked as examples **2. Reason 2: Many walk as enemies of the cross** a. Their end: De-	**C. Pressing On: Marking Those Who Walk as Examples, 3:17-21** 17 Brethren, be followers together of me, and mark them which walk so as ye have us for an ensample. 18 (For many walk, of whom I have told you often, and now tell you even weeping, that they are enemies of the cross of Christ: 19 Whose end is de-	struction, whose God is their belly, and whose glory is in their shame, who mind earthly things.) 20 For our conversation is in heaven; from whence also we look for the Saviour, the Lord Jesus Christ: 21 Who shall change our vile body, that it may be fashioned like unto his glorious body, according to the working whereby he is able even to subdue all things unto himself.	struction b. Their god: Appetite c. Their glory: Shameful d. Their mind: Earthly **3. Reason 3: The believer is a citizen of heaven** a. His life: Heaven centered b. His focus: The return of Christ c. His end: A changed body

Section IV
THE 'PRESSING ON' OF THE CHRISTIAN BELIEVER, Philippians 3:1-21

Study 3: **PRESSING ON: MARKING THOSE WHO WALK AS EXAMPLES**

Text: **Philippians 3:17-21**

Aim: To follow the positive examples set before us, not the negative.

Memory Verse:

"For our conversation [citizenship] is in heaven; whence also we look for the Saviour, the Lord Jesus Christ" (Philippians 3:20).

INTRODUCTION:

The life we live sets a pattern for others to follow. Others are going to follow us no matter what we do. This says something to us, something of critical importance: we must live lives on the highest plane possible. We must set the most dynamic example possible. We must set the most perfect pattern possible for others to follow. But it also says something else: we must follow after those who live on the highest plane of life. We must mark those who walk as examples and follow after the great traits of their lives. We must take those who live as good examples and dissect the traits of their lives, applying those traits to our own lives. This is the subject of the present passage: marking those who walk as examples for us all.

OUTLINE:

1. Reason 1: some walk as good examples (v.17).
2. Reason 2: many walk as enemies of the cross (v.18-19).
3. Reason 3: the believer is a citizen of heaven (v.20-21).

PHILIPPIANS 3:17-21

PERSONAL OUTLINE NOTES

1. REASON 1: SOME WALK AS GOOD EXAMPLES (v.17).

2. REASON 2: MANY WALK AS ENEMIES OF THE CROSS (v.18-19).

3. REASON 3: THE BELIEVER IS A CITIZEN OF HEAVEN (v.20-21).

PHILIPPIANS 3:17-21

SUMMARY:

As you have studied the example of Paul and others, you must learn to:
1. Walk as a good example.
2. Avoid the enemies of the cross.
3. Focus on your heavenly citizenship.

PERSONAL JOURNAL NOTES
(Reflection & Response)

1. The most important thing that I learned from this lesson was:

2. The area that I need to work on the most is:

3. I can apply this lesson to my life by:

4. Closing statement of commitment:

PHILIPPIANS 3:17-21

ADDITIONAL NOTES

	CHAPTER 4 **V. THE SECRET OF PEACE--THE PEACE OF GOD HIMSELF, 4:1-9** **A. The Steps to Peace (Part I): Standing Fast, Unity, Rejoicing, & Gentleness, 4:1-5**		
1. Step 1: Peace comes through standing fast a. The source of strength: Being "in the Lord" b. The encouragement: A brother who cares	Therefore, my brethren dearly beloved and longed for, my joy and crown, so stand fast in the Lord, my dearly beloved.		
2. Step 2: Peace comes through agreement & unity a. The plea: For arguers to agree in the Lord b. The need: The help of a true friend 1) Must help them because they were co-laborers 2) Must help them because their names are in the Book of Life	2 I beseech Euodias,	and beseech Syntyche, that they be of the same mind in the Lord. 3 And I entreat thee also, true yokefellow, help those women which laboured with me in the gospel, with Clement also, and with other my fellowlabourours, whose names are in the book of life.	
3. Step 3: Peace comes through rejoicing continually & repeatedly		4 Rejoice in the Lord always: and again I say, Rejoice.	
4. Step 4: Peace comes through a strong gentleness		5 Let your moderation be known unto all men. The Lord is at hand.	

Section V
THE SECRET OF PEACE—THE PEACE OF GOD HIMSELF,
Philippians 4:1-9

Study 1: THE STEPS TO PEACE (PART I): STANDING FAST, UNITY, REJOICING, & GENTLENESS

Text: Philippians 4:1-5

Aim: To learn the steps to securing peace in your life.

Memory Verse:
"Rejoice in the Lord alway: and again I say rejoice" (Philippians 4:4).

INTRODUCTION:

This passage is speaking to Christian believers, not to unbelievers. Unbelievers do not have peace with God. They reject, question, deny, curse, and oppose God. God feels no peace between Himself and an unbeliever. No matter how mild the unbeliever's questioning and rejection is, it is still questioning and rejection and not peace. But when an unbeliever surrenders his life and accepts God, peace is made between him and God. Peace rules both within and between the person and God. In fact, God causes a flood of peace to surge through the heart and life of the new believer.

The question is this: once we have the peace of God flooding our lives, how do we maintain that peace? How do we keep the peace of God ruling and reigning within our souls? How do we stay aware that God's very own presence is within us—stay aware that the God of peace lives within our very being? This is the discussion of this passage: the steps to peace.

OUTLINE:

1. Step 1: peace comes through standing fast (v.1).
2. Step 2: peace comes through agreement and unity (v.2-3).
3. Step 3: peace comes through rejoicing continually and repeatedly (v.4).
4. Step 4: peace comes through a strong gentleness (v.5).

PHILIPPIANS 4:1-5

PERSONAL OUTLINE NOTES

1. **STEP 1: PEACE COMES THRU STANDING FAST (v.1).**

2. **STEP 2: PEACE COMES THRU AGREEMENT & UNITY (v.2-3).**

3. **STEP 3: PEACE COMES THRU REJOICING CONTINUALLY & REPEATEDLY (v.4).**

PERSONAL OUTLINE NOTES (continued)

4. STEP 4: PEACE COMES THRU A STRONG GENTLENESS (v.5).

SUMMARY:

There are certain steps that are key to achieving peace. You must remember that:
1. Peace comes through standing fast.
2. Peace comes through agreement and unity.
3. Peace comes through rejoicing continually & repeatedly.
4. Peace comes through a strong gentleness.

PHILIPPIANS 4:1-5

PERSONAL JOURNAL NOTES
(Reflection & Response)

1. The most important thing that I learned from this lesson was:

2. The area that I need to work on the most is:

3. I can apply this lesson to my life by:

4. Closing statement of commitment:

PHILIPPIANS 4:6-9

1. Peace comes through prayer a. The charge: Do not worry or be anxious b. The remedy: Prayer 1) About everything 2) With requests 3) With thanksgiving c. The promise: Peace 1) Peace that passes all understanding 2) Peace that keeps our hearts & minds	**B. The Steps to Peace (Part II): Prayer & Positive Thinking, 4:6-9** 6 Be careful for nothing; but in every thing by prayer and supplication with thanksgiving let your requests be made known unto God. 7 And the peace of God, which passeth all understanding, shall keep your hearts and minds through Christ Jesus.	8 Finally, brethren, whatsoever things are true, whatsoever things are honest, whatsoever things are just, whatsoever things are pure, whatsoever things are lovely, whatsoever things are of good report; if there be any virtue, and if there be any praise, think on these things. 9 Those things, which ye have both learned, and received, and heard, and seen in me, do: and the God of peace shall be with you.	**2. Peace comes through positive thinking** a. The charge: Think & do things that are... 1) True 2) Honest 3) Just 4) Pure 5) Lovely 6) Of good report 7) Virtuous 8) Praise-worthy b. The source or power of positive thinking 1) The Word of God 2) Noble examples 3) Self-effort

Section V
THE SECRET OF PEACE:
THE PEACE OF GOD HIMSELF, Philippians 4:1-9

Study 2: THE STEPS TO PEACE (PART II): PRAYER & POSITIVE THINKING

Text: Philippians 4:6-9

Aim: To learn to experience and keep the peace of God.

Memory Verse:

"And the peace of God, which passeth all understanding, shall keep your hearts and minds through Christ Jesus" (Philippians 4:7).

INTRODUCTION:

Once we possess the peace of God, how do we keep and maintain it? How do we keep the *peace of God* ruling and reigning within our hearts? How do we keep a consciousness of God's very own presence within us—an awareness that the "God of peace" lives within our very being? This passage discusses two of the most important steps to possessing peace. Above all other passages, it tells us how to have peace and how to maintain peace. If we will take these two steps, the peace of God will rule and reign in our hearts and lives.

OUTLINE:

1. Peace comes through prayer (v.6-7).
2. Peace comes through positive thinking (v.8-9).

PHILIPPIANS 4:6-9

PERSONAL OUTLINE NOTES

1. PEACE COMES THROUGH PRAYER (v.6-7).

2. PEACE COMES THRU POSITIVE THINKING (v.8-9).

PHILIPPIANS 4:6-9

SUMMARY:

In this lesson, you have learned how to have the peace of God rule and reign in your life. You have discovered that:

1. Peace comes through prayer.
2. Peace comes through positive thinking.

Now would be a good time to renew your commitment to the Lord Jesus by making room for Him in your busy life. Remember:

With His presence comes His peace.

PERSONAL JOURNAL NOTES
(Reflection & Response)

1. The most important thing that I learned from this lesson was:

2. The area that I need to work on the most is:

3. I can apply this lesson to my life by:

4. Closing statement of commitment:

PHILIPPIANS 4:6-9

ADDITIONAL NOTES

	VI. THE APPRECIATION FOR GOOD CHRISTIAN RELATIONSHIPS, 4:10-23 **A. Appreciation: For a Church That Revives Its Sacrificial Giving, 4:10-19**	through Christ which strengtheneth me. 14 Notwithstanding ye have well done, that ye did communicate with my affliction. 15 Now ye Philippians know also, that in the beginning of the gospel, when I departed from Macedonia, no church communicated with me as concerning giving and receiving, but ye only.	necessary because Christ strengthens us through all c. Giving is needed--it is work well done **3. Their giving was distinctive: They were the only church that gave, & they gave consistently**
1. Their giving was revived, & it flourished	10 But I rejoiced in the Lord greatly, that now at the last your care of me hath flourished again; wherein ye were also careful, but ye lacked opportunity.	16 For even in Thessalonica ye sent once and again unto my necessity.	
2. Their giving was not necessary, but it was needed a. Giving is not necessary because God teaches contentment apart from circumstances	11 Not that I speak in respect of want: for I have learned, in whatsoever state I am, therewith to be content. 12 I know both how to be abased, and I know how to abound: every where and in all things I am instructed both to be full and to be hungry, both to abound and to suffer need.	17 Not because I desire a gift: but I desire fruit that may abound to your account. 18 But I have all, and abound: I am full, having received of Epaphroditus the things which were sent from you, an odour of a sweet smell, a sacrifice acceptable, wellpleasing to God.	**4. Their giving was sacrificial, & it was seen & rewarded by God** a. God deposited fruit to their account b. God was well pleased
b. Giving is not	13 I can do all things	19 But my God shall supply all your need according to his riches in glory by Christ Jesus.	c. God promised to supply all their need

Section VI:
THE APPRECIATION FOR GOOD CHRISTIAN RELATIONSHIPS,
Philippians 4:10-23

Study 1: APPRECIATION: FOR A CHURCH THAT REVIVES ITS SACRIFICIAL GIVING

Text: **Philippians 4:10-19**

Aim: To make a genuine pledge to Christ: To always give sacrificially.

Memory Verse:
"But my God shall supply all your need according to His riches in glory by Christ Jesus"(Ph 4:19).

PHILIPPIANS 4:10-19

INTRODUCTION:

What does the Bible say about giving? A lot! This specific passage deals with stewardship, in particular the giving of money to meet the needs of ministers and missions or the spread of the gospel to the world. Remember: Paul is in prison facing the false charge of insurrection against the government. He is facing the death penalty if convicted. The Philippians had heard about his plight, and they had heard how Paul was standing fast and continuing to preach the gospel to everyone who visited him. The church was stirred to do two things: to take up a love offering and to send a man, Epaphroditus, to minister to Paul's needs.

This passage expresses Paul's appreciation for a church that is stirred to revive its interest in missions—stirred to begin giving *once again* to the support of God's ministers world-wide.

OUTLINE:

1. Their giving was revived, and it flourished (v.10).
2. Their giving was not necessary, but it was needed (v.11-14).
3. Their giving was distinctive: they were the only church that gave, and they gave consistently (v.15-16).
4. Their giving was sacrificial, and it was seen and rewarded by God (v.17-19).

PERSONAL OUTLINE NOTES

1. THEIR GIVING WAS REVIVED & IT FLOURISHED (v.10).

2. THEIR GIVING WAS NOT NECESSARY, BUT IT WAS NEEDED (v.11-14).

PERSONAL OUTLINE NOTES (continued)

3. THEIR GIVING WAS DISTINCTIVE: THEY WERE THE ONLY CHURCH THAT GAVE, & THEY GAVE CONSISTENTLY (v.15-16).

4. THEIR GIVING WAS SACRIFICIAL, AND IT WAS SEEN & REWARDED BY GOD (v.17-19).

SUMMARY:

In this lesson, you have learned Christian principles of stewardship, particularly with regards to the giving of money to meet the needs of the gospel ministry.

1. Your giving must be revived and flourish.
2. Your giving is not necessary, but it is needed.
3. You must give and give consistently.
4. Your sacrificial giving will be seen and rewarded by God.

Are you giving sacrificially? Think of the words of this famous hymn, *I Gave My Life For Thee*:

"I gave My life for thee, My precious blood I shed,
That thou might'st ransomed be, And quickened from the dead;
I gave, I gave My life for thee, What hast thou given for Me?" (Text By: Frances R. Havergal).

PHILIPPIANS 4:10-19

PERSONAL JOURNAL NOTES
(Reflection & Response)

1. The most important thing that I learned from this lesson was:

2. The area that I need to work on the most is:

3. I can apply this lesson to my life by:

4. Closing statement of commitment:

	B. Appreciation: For God & For Fellow Christians, 4:20-23
1. God is to be praised as God & as our Father	20 Now unto God and our Father be glory for ever and ever. Amen.
2. Believers are to salute every saint a. Christian leaders are to greet every saint	21 Salute every saint in Christ Jesus. The brethren which are with me greet you.
b. All the saints are to greet other believers, including government officials	22 All the saints salute you, chiefly they that are of Caesar's household.
3. Believers are to wish the grace of our Lord Jesus Christ upon each other	23 The grace of our Lord Jesus Christ be with you all. Amen.

Section VI
THE APPRECIATION FOR GOOD CHRISTIAN RELATIONS,
Philippians 4:10-23

Study 2: **APPRECIATION: FOR GOD & FOR FELLOW CHRISTIANS**

Text: **Philippians 4:20-23**

Aim: To more actively express our appreciation (praise) to God and to fellow believers.

Memory Verse:
"The grace of our Lord Jesus Christ be with you all. Amen" (Ph.4:23).

INTRODUCTION:
Too often we just take things for granted and go about our business without saying a word of thanks to others. Too often we allow our own concerns to get in the way of our being gracious, thankful, and appreciative. This passage gives us a dynamic challenge. We should be far more active in expressing appreciation to God and to fellow believers.

OUTLINE:
1. God is to be praised as God and as our Father (v.20).
2. Believers are to salute every saint (v.21-22).
3. Believers are to wish the grace of our Lord Jesus Christ upon each other (v.23).

PHILIPPIANS 4:20-23

PERSONAL OUTLINE NOTES

1. GOD IS TO BE PRAISED AS GOD AND AS OUR FATHER (v.20).

2. BELIEVERS ARE TO SALUTE EVERY SAINT (v.21-22).

3. BELIEVERS ARE TO WISH THE GRACE OF OUR LORD JESUS CHRIST UPON EACH OTHER (v.23).

PHILIPPIANS 4:20-23

SUMMARY:

It is crucial that you worship God properly and learn to do a better job of appreciating other believers. Remember, you must:

1. Praise God as God and as your Father.
2. Salute every saint.
3. Wish the grace of our Lord Jesus Christ upon each other.

PERSONAL JOURNAL NOTES
(Reflection & Response)

1. The most important thing that I learned from this lesson was:

2. The area that I need to work on the most is:

3. I can apply this lesson to my life by:

4. Closing statement of commitment:

PHILIPPIANS 4:20-23

ADDITIONAL NOTES

PHILIPPIANS

ADDITIONAL NOTES

ADDITIONAL NOTES

PHILIPPIANS

ADDITIONAL NOTES

PHILIPPIANS

ADDITIONAL NOTES

PURPOSE STATEMENT

LEADERSHIP MINISTRIES WORLDWIDE

exists to equip ministers, teachers, and laymen in their understanding, preaching, and teaching of God's Word by publishing and distributing worldwide *The Preacher's Outline & Sermon Bible*® and related *Outline* Bible materials, to reach & disciple men, women, boys, and girls for Jesus Christ.

•MISSION STATEMENT•

1. To make the Bible so understandable - its truth so clear and plain - that men and women everywhere, whether teacher or student, preacher or hearer, can grasp its Message and receive Jesus Christ as Savior; and...
2. To place the Bible in the hands of all who will preach and teach God's Holy Word, verse by verse, precept by precept, regardless of the individual's ability to purchase it.

The ***Outline*** Bible materials have been given to LMW for printing and especially distribution worldwide at/below cost, by those who remain anonymous. One fact, however, is as true today as it was in the time of Christ:

• The Gospel is free, but the cost of taking it is not •

LMW depends on the generous gifts of Believers with a heart for Him and a love and burden for the lost. They help pay for the printing, translating, and placing ***Outline*** Bible materials in the hands and hearts of those worldwide who will present God's message with clarity, authority and understanding beyond their own.

LMW was incorporated in the state of Tennessee in July 1992 and received IRS 501(c) 3 non-profit status in March 1994. LMW is an international, nondenominational mission organization. All proceeds from USA sales, along with donations from donor partners, go 100% into underwriting our translation and distribution projects of ***Outline*** Bible materials to preachers, church & lay leaders, and Bible students around the world.

5/97

PO Box 21310 - Chattanooga, TN 37424 • (423) 855-2181 • FAX (423) 855-8616
• E-Mail 74152.616@compuserve.com — Web site: http://www.outlinebible.org •

LEADERSHIP MINISTRIES WORLDWIDE
The Preacher's Outline & Sermon Bible
Sharing
The OUTLINED BIBLE
With the World!